D1394299

The Wee Book of

ABERDEEN

Norman Adams

Black & White Publishing

First published 2004
by Black & White Publishing Ltd
99 Giles Street, Edinburgh EH6 6BZ

ISBN 1 84502 007 3

Textual copyright © Norman Adams
Photographs on pp. 5, 9, 13, 19, 23, 31, 33, 35, 37, 41, 43, 49, 57, 61, 71, 75, 77, 79, 81,
83, 85, 87 and 89 © D. C. Thomson & Co. Ltd, 2004
Photographs on pp. 7, 11, 15, 17, 21, 39, 45, 47, 59, 63, 65,
67 and 93 © Aberdeen City Council (Publicity and Promotions Department)
Photographs on pp. 25, 27, 29, 51, 53, 55, 73 and 95 © Aberdeen City Council
(Library and Information Services)
Photograph on p. 69 © Grant-Photo, Inverurie
Photograph on p. 91 reproduced by kind permission of Dr Adam Watson
Photograph on p. 96 reproduced by kind permission of Michael Marshall
Front cover photographs: Union Terrace Gardens © Aberdeen City Council (Publicity and Promotions
Department); Archibald Simpson's © Aberdeen City Council (Publicity and Promotions Department);
sculpture behind St Nicholas House reproduced by kind permission of Michael Marshall
Back cover photograph: Town House and Mannie Well reproduced
by kind permission of Michael Marshall

Also by Norman Adams
Blood and Granite – True Crime from Aberdeen

A CIP catalogue record for this book is available from The British Library.

Printed and bound in Spain by Bookprint, S.L., Barcelona.

INTRODUCTION

Aberdonians have the ability to laugh at themselves. No library should be complete without a well-thumbed copy of the Aberdeen joke book with its famous postcard of a deserted Union Street on Flag Day. The city's own master of mirth, Harry Gordon (1893–1957), gleefully spread the reputation of the canny Aberdonian and the Scotland the What? comedy team later injected their own brand of satire to keep the self-deprecating humour alive.

But Aberdeen is no mean city – and this is no joke book. As you turn the pages, its evocative images will bring a host of happy memories flooding back – a day at the Timmer Market fifty years ago, Fergie's Red Army, a 'dook' at the Beach Baths or the 'Puffin' Billies' at Hazlehead.

Aberdonians have also suffered the worst of times. There were the war-torn years and the decline of famous industries. The city is still recognised as the Granite City yet there are no major working quarries left in the area. Although the port still has an important fishing role, the huge local trawler fleet and the shipyards that built it are now a distant memory. Despite the first oil bubble bursting in the mid 1980s, the oil industry continues to dominate the local economy. But, even after thirty years of oil, the guy wearing a Stetson is more likely to be a line-dancer than a Texan.

Farmer and author John R Allan described Aberdeen granite as an 'unconquerable stone'. Its citizens are also unconquerable and their individualism, culture, humour and enterprising spirit has made their city what it is.

Norman Adams

Balloons bob in the balmy air on a special day at the Market Stance off Justice Street. The Timmer Market in Coronation Year 1953 is in full swing and folk are drawn to stalls laden with all kinds of goodies. Dodging split peas fired from pea-shooters by mischievous boys was all part of the fun. The traditional August market, an offshoot of a medieval fair, was held in the nearby Castlegate until 1934. At this time, the wooden wares were mainly red-painted toys, spurtles, tattie mashers, cradles and stools.

The Timmer Market has now returned to its roots in the Castlegate and it still lives up to its name as these wooden flowerpot figures testify. Open-air fairs catering for local and exotic tastes are often held in Union Street. In one weekend, a continental market, selling everything from Belgian chocolates to German beer, attracted 120,000 shoppers. It just goes to show that the shopping mall hasn't completely taken over from the traditional market just yet.

Aberdonians walk the Castlegate in the footsteps of royalty and rogues. It is documented that Mary, Queen of Scots, King James VI and Charles II, known as the 'Merrie Monarch', all visited the area and the present Queen is no stranger to this place. The Merrie Monarch's scandalous behaviour with his mistress at his lodgings in 1650 drew a sharp rebuke from the Kirk.

In earlier times, petty criminals were ridiculed at the Mercat Cross. The burgh hangman found grim work at the gallows at the door of the Tolbooth, a former jail, courthouse and town hall. It is now a museum. Its weathercock is prominent in this 1969 view.

The architect of the Salvation Army Citadel, with its impressive baronial turrets, was inspired by Balmoral Castle.

Demeter, the Greek goddess of the corn, flanked by a lion and a horn of plenty, casts her bountiful gaze on the Castlegate from her throne above the portico of a bank, on the north-west corner of King Street and Castle Street. The bank with its Corinthian columns is now a pub and bears the name of its architect, Archibald Simpson. The Granite City had a reputation for moving its statues to different locations but this one, sculpted by James Giles and the city's only terracotta effigy, has been here since the middle of the nineteenth century.

In another age, the popular New Inn stood on this spot. After receiving the Freedom of the City in 1773, Dr Samuel Johnson and his biographer James Boswell stayed here. Robert Burns also stayed in the inn but he couldn't have been very impressed as he called Aberdeen 'a lazy town'.

The baronial beauty of the Town House clock tower and the neighbouring Tolbooth make an imposing background.

Scots author Eric Linklater wrote eloquently of 'Jimmy Hay's Restaurant', a name that stuck with an older generation long after it became the equally popular Royal Athenaeum, overlooking the Castlegate. But, in August 1973, fire destroyed its lofty dining room which bore the gilded motto:

He that drinks well, sleeps well.
He that sleeps well, works well.
He that works well, eats well.

Five years later, work began on restoring the gracious Georgian building. The ground floor is now the appropriately-named Athenaeum Bar and the upper floors are offices.

The statue in front of the gutted restaurant is another landmark, The Mannie Well, which originally stood at the opposite end of the Castlegate. The well was removed to The Green in 1852. During its time there, it was known as The Mannie o' the Green and, in 1972, it was flitted back to the Castlegate.

The electric tramcar was king of the road during this Friday rush hour on Union Street in March 1930. Glaswegians had their 'shooglies' and Aberdonians boasted of their 'carries', whose eye-catching green and cream livery was a familiar sight. Corporation charabancs, motor cars and cyclists jostle for position on a street paved with granite 'cassies' as pedestrians hurry about their business. The momentum would be stepped up a gear that same year with the arrival of double-decker buses.

Here, we are looking east towards the Citadel and the Ionic column at the left-hand side is part of the centrepiece of architect John Smith's handsome 1829 façade to the St Nicholas Church graveyard.

In the early history of Aberdeen's public transport system, the Corporation Tramways was determined no passenger would get a free ride. So, before the First World War, a pay-as-you-enter double-decker tramcar was introduced on several routes. It was the first scheme of its kind in Europe. A conductor collected fares as passengers were admitted at the rear of the tram. After the outbreak of the Second World War, 'streamliners' appeared in the streets. A larger and later version is seen approaching the Union Bridge in the 1950s.

The corporation failed to sell the Wishaw-built trams, nicknamed 'Blackpool Balloons', to Blackpool, and the city's tramcar fleet, which began with the introduction of horse-drawn trams in 1874, was destined to end in ignominy.

By the mid 1950s, Aberdeen Town Council decided the city's tramcars had fallen out of fashion. The end was in sight when the Rosemount line was axed on a dreary November night in 1954. But the final run did not go as planned. The procession to the terminus was headed by tram No. 1, which had been specially rebuilt in horse-drawn car form for the tramway silver jubilee celebrations in 1924. The two Clydesdales were unable to haul the tram, driven by Lord Provost Graham, on an incline. So the horseless vehicle and its passengers (including two future Lord Provosts) suffered the indignity of being pushed by the tram behind.

No. 1, the city's sole surviving tram, can be seen at the Grampian Transport Museum in Alford.

Seventy thousand people waved goodbye as the last tram paraded down Union Street that sad Saturday night in May 1958. But few, including the author, who were on that final journey, guessed what the city fathers had in mind for the surviving fleet of 'carries'. Nine days later, in the early hours of Monday 12 May, the Beach Links was lit up by a funeral pyre. Only a handful of spectators, mainly folk from Constitution Street who had been rudely wakened by the passing trams, watched as a scrap merchant borrowed a match to set ablaze paraffin-soaked tramcar No. 137.

On a sun-splashed day, crowds line Union Street to watch the 1984 Aberdeen Festival Parade roll by. The main thoroughfare has captured the hearts and minds of Aberdonians for more than 200 years. It is a street of memories, pageantry, romance, laughter and a few tears. The street has rolled out the red carpet for famous people receiving the Freedom of the City, including Rowland Hill, founder of the penny post, explorer Henry Stanley, philanthropist Andrew Carnegie and wartime leader Sir Winston Churchill. In 1956 the accolade was awarded to the north-east's own regiment, the Gordon Highlanders.

Queen Victoria seems to stare down her nose at the folk scurrying beneath her granite plinth at the corner of Union Street and St Nicholas Street. For generations folk would arrange to meet at 'the Queen'. Her bronze effigy marked the end of the line for trams from Woodside.

St Nicholas Street and George Street offered a wide range of shopping down the years from department stores like Isaac Benzies to Morrison's Economic Stores – better known as Raggie Morrison's – where there were always bargains to be had. But these shops have gone now and shopping malls have replaced them.

After seventy years, Victoria herself was unceremoniously removed in January 1964 to Queen's Cross where she now gazes in the direction of her beloved Balmoral.

Here's a peep into the time before these shady stretches of St Nicholas Street and the historic Netherkirkgate were cleared away. We catch a glimpse of turreted Benholm's Lodging, better known as the Wallace Tower, which was a popular howff before it was removed, stone by stone, to Tillydrone in the early 1960s. Built 280 years after Wallace's death, the tower actually has no connection with the Scottish patriot but wide-eyed children were told that the carving of a knight in one of the tower's recesses depicted William Wallace and his faithful hound. The carving was most probably a tombstone from the nearby St Nicholas Church, also known as the Mither Kirk.

Mind you, comedian Harry Gordon claimed he 'hid a drink wi' him [Wallace] inside the Wallace Toor'. It stood at the head of Putachieside, now Carnegie's Brae, part of the ancient highway into Aberdeen from the south.

The swirl of their green and yellow tartan was a familiar sight during the years the Gordon Highlanders made Aberdeen their regimental home. In 1935, the year the regiment moved from Castlehill, behind the Castlegate, to Gordon Barracks at Bridge of Don, this contingent marched to a Union Street cinema with pipes and drums at their head. The Picture House featured The Iron Duke *with veteran actor George Arliss in the title role of the Duke of Wellington. It was a rare treat. The dull stutter of gunfire from the firing range at Black Dog reminded civilians there was more to soldiering than going to the flicks.*

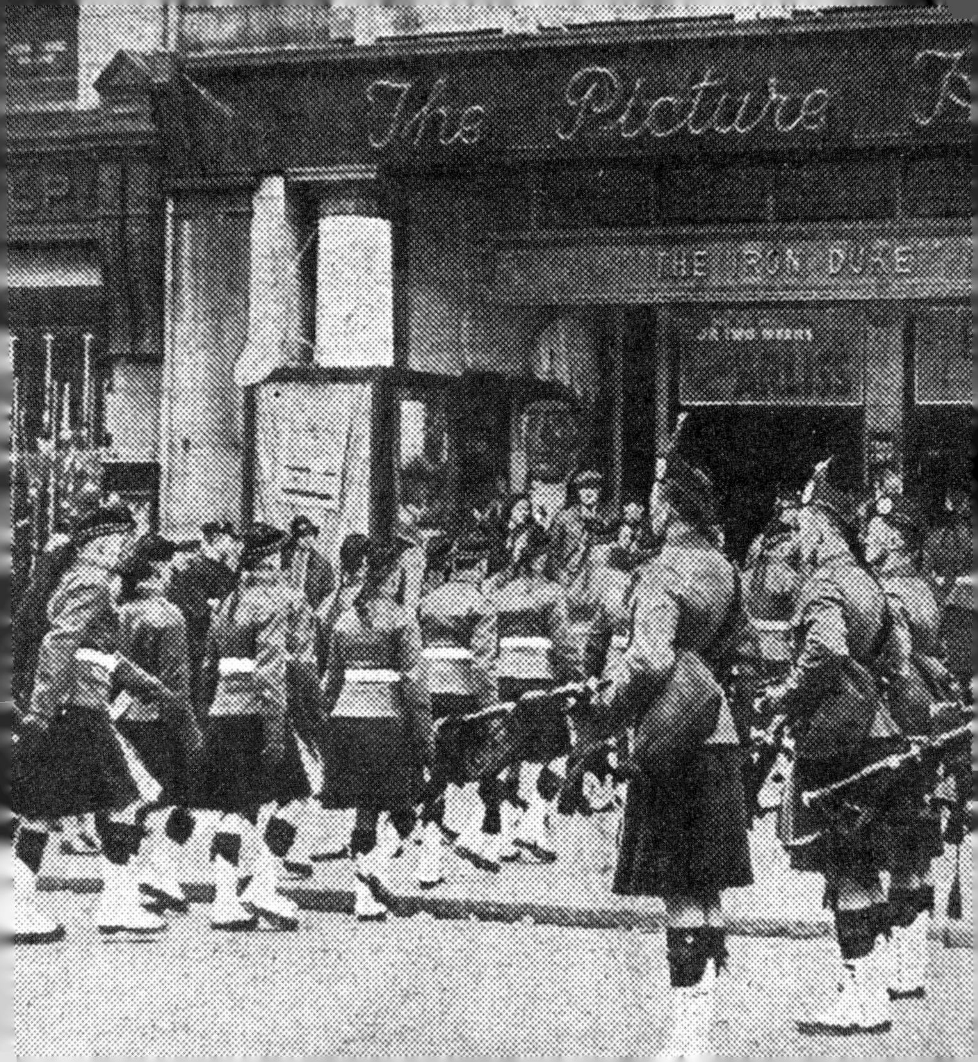
The Picture
THE IRON DUKE

When the art deco Capitol Cinema opened in 1933, a resident organist and live shows added to the glamour. The tradition was resurrected in the 1950s and 1960s when the popularity of television began to hit cinema takings. To buck the trend, the Capitol became a venue for pop concerts, attracting big names like Tommy Steele, Dusty Springfield, Cliff Richard and the Bay City Rollers.

The Rolling Stones proved a sensation during two visits in the 1960s. In June 1965, fears of rowdyism by fans were unwarranted although a newspaper reporter was frog-marched from the auditorium for overstaying his welcome. Fans queued for tickets in a deluge for the Stones' third visit in 1982. The show was a sell-out and tickets changed hands for three-figure sums, a serious amount of money to an Aberdonian.

Marischal College commands centre stage in this pilot's-eye view of frost-glazed roofs and streets during the early oil boom years. The pepper pot tower of the Arts Centre in King Street (lower left), St Nicholas House and the clock spire of St Nicholas Church, the Mither Kirk, (both upper left) are well-known landmarks.

But the landscape of this 1980 overview was about to undergo a major facelift and, before the end of the decade, St Nicholas Street and George Street had undergone drastic surgery to make room for two shopping malls.

And now the seat of learning itself faces change. It is earmarked for development but the Mitchell Hall, named after a shipbuilding benefactor, will still play host to the university's ceremonial activities.

32

Provost Skene's House was named after a former owner, Sir George Skene of Rubislaw, a wealthy merchant and Provost of Aberdeen in the seventeenth century. An older generation would have known it as Cumberland House, from the enforced six-week occupancy by the Duke of Cumberland who was on his way to Culloden. In later years, it became a House of Refuge and then the Victoria Lodging House.

It was facing demolition until, in 1938, Queen Elizabeth took a personal interest in its restoration. By 1953, it had been returned to its former grandeur when these council workmen added the final touches to the garden court in anticipation of the official opening appropriately by Her Majesty who, by then, was Queen Mother.

It's fitting that the city's oldest dwelling, Provost Ross's House in the Shiprow, overlooking the harbour, is now part of the Aberdeen Maritime Museum. The house, built in 1593, was owned by a succession of wealthy shipping merchants, including John Ross of Arnage, Provost from 1710–12, who died on a business trip to Amsterdam.

The house fell on hard times in the mid-twentieth century and was earmarked for demolition by the Town Council. But, with the Queen Mother's support, the National Trust for Scotland was able to save it and restoration began in November 1952. Soon after it was reopened in 1954, the Trust took a call from the Inland Revenue inquiring if Provost Ross was still in residence! This undated shot was obviously taken before traffic wardens were introduced.

Aberdeen prides itself on a stirring maritime heritage
that includes building speedy clippers for the Australian
wool trade. The most famous, Thermopylae, *was a*
record-breaker and she achieved this with the help of
her streamlined stem, the famous 'Aberdeen bow', which
was invented by a local shipbuilder.

People were given a taste of those heady days when
contestants in the Cutty Sark Tall Ships' Race made the
city their port of call on two memorable occasions in
1991 and 1997. Thousands thronged the quaysides,
bristling with masts, to enjoy the sights and sounds.
And, when the time came to set sail, crews left with the
toast of Bon Accord ringing in their ears:

Happy to meet.
Sorry to part.
Happy to meet again!

Queen Victoria caught Aberdeen on the hop when the Royal Yacht Victoria and Albert *docked a day early for the monarch's first-ever visit in September 1848. She and her consort were about to spend their first holiday at Balmoral. Despite not being fully prepared for the visit, Aberdeen rose to the occasion magnificently.*

And the welcome was equally rousing when Britannia *slipped into port with the Duke of Edinburgh on board in 1954, the year after Queen Elizabeth II's coronation. After a three-week Canadian tour, the Duke joined his family who were holidaying at Balmoral. The Royal Yacht was a regular visitor to the city, conveying its royal passengers north for their annual stay on Deeside, until it found a retirement berth at Leith.*

Over the years, considerate boatmen would use sign language when tying up the great ship to save disturbing the royals. And, to prevent an accident during disembarkation, crane tracks on the quayside were temporarily filled with cement.

*The clock tower of the nineteenth-century Harbour Office
looms above tall-rigged fishing boats that would not
have been out of place in the Victorian era. The white-
walled vessels, tied up in the Upper Dock in 1948,
netted fish in their home waters around the Faroe
Islands before heading for Aberdeen to sell their catches.
At sea you could hear the chug-chug of their diesel
engines miles before they came into view.*

*In August 1954, a Faroese amateur football squad
arrived by fishing boat to play their first-ever game on
grass. Aberdeen's flamboyant referee Peter Craigmyle
was behind the trip.*

*Compare this tranquil scene with the hustle and bustle
of an oil boom dock more than half a century later.*

From a lofty viewpoint, the brightly painted oil-industry supply ships fuss around the harbour like toy boats in murky bath water. But, from close quarters on the quayside at the Upper Dock, they are floating giants with names to match – Northern Canyon, Highland Eagle *and* Highland Courage.

The port has come a long way since its first official mention in history. The harbour board, established in 1136 by King David I of Scotland, is Britain's oldest business.

And, talking of records, the Mither Kirk, whose clock spire can be seen in the background, houses the largest carillon in Britain. It's comprised of forty-eight bells, which were recast and rehung in 1952. Because of defects, the old bells had remained silent since their installation in 1887 for Queen Victoria's Golden Jubilee the previous century.

Prince Philip disembarked from the Royal Yacht, sniffed the tang wafting from the fish market and quipped that he always knew when he was in Aberdeen. His off-the-cuff remark is still topical despite the problems that have plagued Scottish fishermen. The Victorian red-brick fish market is no more but Aberdeen is still a leading European centre for the landing and processing of fish. Catches at smaller ports are sent here for auction and the harbour also handles imports of chilled and frozen fish for processing locally.

The markets at Palmerston and Commercial quays have been brought up to food-hall standards. But, when our photo was taken on market day, all of that was in the future.

In the 1950s, a workman, who lassoed fish baskets that had been dropped into the harbour, was nicknamed Roy Rogers, after the Western movie star.

There was a time when schoolboys knew the registration number of every Aberdeen trawler as intimately as they knew their stamp or cigarette card collection. In the mid 1970s, when this shot of Point Law was taken, 100 local boats sailed from the port. Twelve years later, that number had shrunk to just six. Now, the traditional Aberdeen trawler fleet has been confined to history.

The industry began humbly enough when, in 1882, a former Dublin paddle tug, Toiler, *landed three boxes of haddock which had been caught after just a short trip round the bay. The catch fetched thirty-seven shillings, a tidy sum in those days. The leaky tub was sold at a loss and later sank in the Moray Firth. Curiously, her successor,* North Star, *fished up* Toiler's *oak trawl beam and it was later erected in the garden of trawl owner William Pyper, who was one of the crew on the* Toiler's *maiden trip.*

The war changed lives at home forever. Gas masks were issued to all ages, with portable hoods for babies and red Mickey Mouse masks for toddlers. Food and fuel rationing and the blackout became a way of life. Strategic buildings, such as police stations, first aid posts, hospitals and schools, were protected by walls of sandbags. The harbour was enclosed by a stockade of barbed wire stretching from the Victoria Bridge to the bottom of Waterloo Quay. No one was allowed entry without a pass.

Another wartime measure was to have traffic signs and kerb edges painted with zebra stripes to guide pedestrians and motorists at night. These markings can be seen on the lamp posts on the quayside where a goods train is heading for the yard at Waterloo.

Where were you when the siren blew? Because of its close proximity to occupied Norway, Aberdeen was the most frequently bombed city in Scotland. The majority of attacks were carried out by lone tip-and-run raiders. The most devastating raid happened on 21 April 1943 when twenty-nine Dorniers dropped forty-one tons of bombs on a virtually unprotected city. The week before, most of the anti-aircraft guns had been sent south where the Blitz was reducing English cities to brick dust. The hour-long raid, a reprisal for an RAF attack on Hamburg, cost the lives of ninety-seven people with 235 wounded.

A Berlin magazine published sketches by a German pilot that claimed to show a nose-gunner's-eye view of a flak tower, sprouting guns. In reality, it was the water-cooling tower at Berryden dairy.

Here, we can see workmen filling bomb craters in Clifton Road after a 1941 raid.

The magic of the silver screen has worked its spell on Aberdonians for generations. Before the outbreak of the Second World War, the city boasted nineteen cinemas, almost all of which offered a complete change of programme twice a week. The Casino, affectionately known as the 'Casash', brought an exotic touch to the narrow streets of the East End when it opened in 1916.

In the 1940s, it was showing Hollywood musicals to brighten lives during those dark wartime days. It was demolished over thirty years ago. At the same time, its neighbour, the Star Picture Palace, was also reduced to rubble. From the silent era to the early talkies youngsters were admitted to the 'Starrie' in return for a jam jar or two!

Old Torry, once part of Kincardineshire, received a Royal Charter in 1494 and its fisherfolk fiercely retained a separate identity from the citizens 'ower the watter'. They probably thought they were doing the city a favour by agreeing to become part of Aberdeen in 1891.

Fishwives with creels on their backs would collect shellfish and seaweed from the Bay of Nigg while their menfolk went small-line fishing for haddock, codling and whiting. The harvest of the sea was then taken into the city and sold at The Green.

Here in Fore Close, with its characteristic flight of fore-stairs, a housewife collects her daily pinta while bairns caper and a dog chases pigeons. Scenes like these vanished in 1974 when the village at the mouth of the Dee was bulldozed, amid great controversy, to make room for Shell UK's oil-rig supply base.

Robert Louis Stevenson wrote that, whenever he smelt salt water, he knew he was close to one of the works of his ancestors. The famous Torry landmark, Girdleness Lighthouse, is one of ninety-seven lighthouses his family designed and built around the Scottish coast. His grandfather, Robert, designed it and James Gibb of Aberdeen built it. The astronomer royal of the time described it as the best lighthouse he'd ever seen.

Below the lighthouse, a stormy sea lashes Greyhope Bay. It was here that the whaling ship Oscar *foundered on April Fool's Day 1813. Only two of the crew of forty-three survived. That disaster and subsequent wrecks prompted the building of the lighthouse. In 1991, the light was no longer manned, its sweeping beam becoming automated.*

Wags like to say that William Wallace, atop his 200-ton pedestal of Correnie granite, is directing patrons to His Majesty's. But the statue of 'Braveheart' overlooked the Denburn Valley long before a single stone of the theatre was laid. No one really knows what the Scottish hero looked like but this effigy, which was originally earmarked for the Duthie Park Mound, was intended to represent him snubbing the English ambassadors before routing the Auld Enemy at the Battle of Stirling Bridge in September 1297.

In December 1906 – eighteen years after Wallace took up his stance at the end of Union Terrace – the good and the great of Edwardian Aberdeen were greeted by theatre manager Harry Adair Nelson on opening night of Little Red Riding Hood, *an operatic pantomime.*

Aberdeen has worn many caps and titles. Some think of it as the Granite City, to others it is Global Energy City but, for many, it is the Rose City. Its record in the Britain in Bloom competition is second to none. Aberdeen won the Scottish cities' trophy so often the city was given it to keep in 1988. The smallest park, Johnston Gardens in Seafield, was named best public park in the UK two years ago.

And then, nestling in the Denburn Valley, there's Union Terrace Gardens. The city-centre stretches of the Denburn, where ducks once swam, were culverted in the mid nineteenth century. The floral civic coat of arms, with its brave leopards, the Wallace statue, His Majesty's Theatre and domed St Mark's Church all add grandeur to a summer day. But the gardens have seen better times and need revitalising. Happily, though, property speculators and developers have, so far, failed to get their hands on the area.

*When the fiery message, 'Long Live Miss Duthie',
illuminated the night sky over the Dee on 27 September
1883, Aberdonians celebrated in style. They had braved
torrential rain as Elizabeth Crombie Duthie handed
Princess Beatrice, Queen Victoria's youngest daughter, a
silver key to open the new Duthie Park, her gift to the
citizens. The park is not the city's oldest or largest park,
but it holds a special place in everyone's heart. Miss
Duthie died eighteen months after the park opened.*

*A popular spot in the park was the Palm House, a
domed building constructed of St Petersburg redwood. It
was erected in 1899 but demolished seventy years later
to make way for the Winter Gardens. This aluminium
and glass building has since been refurbished and
renamed in memory of David Welch who, during his
time as the city's parks director, turned Aberdeen into
Scotland's floral capital.*

*Now here's a real blast from the past – 'Puffin' Billies'
on parade at the popular Steam Festival in Hazlehead
Park. Steam rollers and vintage tractors and lorries with
resounding names, like* The Highlander *and* Hielan'
Laddie, *chugged, reeked and whistled as they circuited
the grassy arena. The show, which was inaugurated in
the late 1960s by the Bon Accord Steam Engine Club,
became the biggest annual rally in Scotland. Eleven
years ago Scotland's oldest preserved traction engine,*
Auld Charlie, *celebrated its centenary at Hazlehead.*

On 6 July 1988, 167 men on the Piper Alpha oil platform lost their lives in the world's worst offshore disaster. On a hot, cloudless day, on the third anniversary of the tragedy, bereaved families, survivors, rescuers and friends watched as the Queen Mother unveiled the Piper Alpha Memorial in the spectacular rose garden at Hazlehead Park. She then moved among the crowd to offer words of compassion and encouragement.

Ironically, the memorial's creator, Sue Jane Taylor, had sketched and painted some of the crewmen of Piper Alpha during a visit to the platform the year before the disaster happened.

The Granite City became the Beleaguered City in May 1964 when an infected tin of corned beef caused the biggest typhoid outbreak (504 cases) in Britain for a generation. Social and sports events were cancelled, schools and public baths were shut and summer visitors shunned the city. The all-clear was given a month later and the Queen received a rapturous welcome when she paid a surprise visit. At the City Hospital there were smiles from recuperating patients as they communicated with their families through closed windows.

Dr Ian MacQueen's annual report differed in appearance from his other reports as Medical Officer of Health in that the cover was entirely black. The late, good doctor certainly had a strong sense of humour.

In the late twenties and thirties, the beach amusement park was a big draw and the scenic railway was a great favourite with kids of all ages. On a clear day you could almost see forever from the top – but that was before the carriages plunged down the stomach-churning final lap.

The railway, built by American showman John Henry Iles, became a towering inferno when fire broke out on the tallest part of the timber structure on 5 December 1940. Three firemen were hurt while fighting the blaze.

The city's first fun ride, Duckworth's switchback railway, entertained Victorian crowds.

The beach is still a haven for fun- and thrill-seekers and is home to Scotland's largest permanent funfair.

Years before they migrated to Mediterranean hot spots, holidaymakers in the early 1950s were wooed to Aberdeen by travel posters singing the praises of 'The Silver City with the Golden Sands'. During the Glasgow Fair, the famous golden beach was turned dark with people. Adult sun-seekers never adopted a devil-may-care attitude to getting a tan so naked flesh was restricted to bare arms and legs.

In this 1952 shot, some adults take their ease on deckchairs while youngsters paddle in the surf. The salmon nets were best avoided at low tide. A few hardy swimmers, determined to be first in, would lead the charge with the battle cry, 'Last een in's a hairy kipper!'

Who's for a 'dook' in the Beach Baths? The red-brick Victorian bathing station on the esplanade provided salt-water bathing as well as spray, plunge and shower baths for both men and women – in separate wings of course. There was a gallery for spectators and changing booths were just a few steps from the edge of the pool. In the 1950s, attendants allowed daring youths to walk under water with the aid of a crude diving helmet – a pail suitably weighted to keep it in position! The baths were greatly reduced in size by the time this photo was taken in 1972, the year they were demolished.

But all is not lost. Swimmers today have the choice of the art deco Bon Accord Baths in Justice Mill Lane or the Beach Leisure Centre with its flumes and wave pool.

Long before today's younger generation found fun in such exotic places as Disneyland, their mums and dads let their childish imaginations run riot in this adventure playground at the Beach. Here they could sail the Seven Seas on a three-master, dig for pirate treasure in the sandpit or go yachting on the pond – though the boy on the left looks as if he may have taken the plunge while fully clothed!

There were climbing nets and tunnels, a lighthouse and a train that an active mind might put to use in a Wild West hold-up. It was often the simplest of pleasures that forged such childhood memories in the summer of 1963.

'C'm awa the Dons!' Aberdonians have supported their senior club since 1903 when three local teams, Orion, Victoria United and the original Aberdeen, amalgamated. The new Aberdeen FC adopted the original Aberdeen's white strip, their nickname, 'The Whites', and, more importantly, the team's ground, Pittodrie Park. By the time the club was admitted into the Scottish First Division in 1905, after two frustrating years in lower leagues, it had new colours, black and gold stripes, and a nickname to match, 'The Wasps'. They became 'The Dons' – probably shortened from 'The Aberdonians' – before the First World War and switched to the now familiar red jerseys six months before the outbreak of the Second World War.

In this view from the Beach End in 1966, the famous gasometer looms above the south terracing and Scotland's first all-seated stadium was still in the future.

It was a night to remember – Wednesday 11 May 1983. The Dons, cheered on by around 14,000 rain-sodden fans, beat Real Madrid 2-1 to lift the European Cup-Winners' Cup. On touchdown at Aberdeen Airport next day, the Gothenburg heroes rode in an open-topped bus to Pittodrie through streets thronged with well-wishers.

Before his team flew out to Sweden, manager Alex Ferguson had wished bon voyage to 500 supporters who sailed for Gothenburg on the P&O ferry, St Clair. He had promised them he would greet them with the cup on their return. When the ship docked, Alex shook hands with every fan as they disembarked and player Mark McGhee added his thanks.

The fans were great ambassadors for the city and the club. Not even a light bulb on board the ferry was broken during the memorable trip.

The big parade of 1983 rolled on. Despite being pipped for the Scottish Premier League title on the Saturday after Gothenburg, a jaded Dons side later retained the Scottish Cup, for the second year running, with an extra-time goal against Rangers at Hampden. Even though they won, Ferguson was unhappy with their performance and publicly rebuked them. But it is a measure of the man that, next morning, he apologised to his players before they set off for home and their second victory parade in ten days. Before the New Year, the Dons had added another piece of silverware to their trophy room after beating Hamburg in the two-leg European Super Cup.

Ferguson, now Sir Alex, has successfully managed Manchester United since 1986, becoming one of the game's greatest managers. He was made a freeman of the City of Aberdeen in March 1999.

The blink of a camera shutter captures this evocative image of the Brig o' Balgownie in winter 1953. Artists and poets have also been inspired by the bridge which carried travellers north from Aberdeen from medieval times to the nineteenth century. However, a prophecy, attributed to the Border seer, Thomas the Rhymer, warned:

Brig o' Balgownie, wicht [meaning 'strong'] is thy wa',
Wi' a wife's ae son an' a mare's ae foal
Doon shalt thou fa'.

Another poet, Lord Byron, while at school in Aberdeen, feared the prophecy. As his mother's only son he would gaze into the 'Black Neuk Pot', a forty-foot hole in the riverbed on the upstream side of the brig, and expect the worst. But he obviously didn't cross on the only foal of a mare.

Shrewd investment in a seventeenth-century fund to preserve the brig amassed enough revenue to build the present Bridge of Don. Situated downstream from the old brig, it carries a steady flow of traffic today.

Aberdeen University Rectorial Elections give students a chance to let their hair down. In the past, things got pretty boisterous when a rector was installed. In 1910, Prime Minister Asquith's carriage was tossed into the harbour. Luckily, the new rector was not a passenger. In 1955, police were forced to draw batons. Here, three years later, a snow-flecked John M Bannerman, politician, Gaelic scholar and former Scottish rugby internationalist, and his supporters were pelted with snowballs by rivals as they hurried from Marischal College to celebrate in the Kirkgate Bar, still a popular student howff.

High jinks by students during Charities Week, the Rectorial Elections or some other stunt inevitably grabbed the headlines when citizens awoke to find a skeleton, banner or chamber pot fixed to the spire of Marischal College's Mitchell Tower. On a cold February morning in 1951, two zoology students, Adam Watson and Bill Jenkins, were driven by a reporter from the now defunct local weekly newspaper, Bon-Accord, *to Rubislaw Quarry. There, they hung a somewhat insubstantial dummy, dressed in a student's red toga, on a cableway stretched across the 500-ft deep, snow-dashed chasm. Although the pair of daredevils wore safety slings, the stunt – whose aim was to promote a campaign to bring back the red togas for students – was perilous. Their clothes stuck to the greasy cable and hoarfrost numbed their fingers. But they succeeded in their task even though, as Adam's dramatic picture shows, the dummy had come adrift before Bill reached safety.*

They began quarrying the grey granite from a rocky wart at Rubislaw at a time when it lay in the open countryside to the west of Aberdeen. London's decision, 250 years ago, to have its streets paved with granite clinched Aberdeen's reputation for producing the durable stone. The quarry, said to be the largest artificial hole in Europe, provided the raw material for famous buildings at home and overseas. The city's Union Bridge – Telford's leap of faith – is still the world's largest single-span stone bridge.

There are no major granite quarries left in the area and, of the ninety granite merchants that existed before the First World War, only two now survive.

Since it closed in 1971, the quarry at Rubislaw which gave birth to the Granite City has filled with water and resembles a black lagoon – a sad memorial to a once famous industry. Today, oil industry offices and luxury flats perch around its rim.

The twin spires of St Machar's Cathedral in Old Aberdeen are a fond and familiar landmark. In the sixth century, St Machar was commanded by St Columba to build a church on the banks of a river where its twists and turns resembled a bishop's staff. The Irish missionary established the original church on the River Don about 580 AD. The legend of its founding seems less fanciful from the air as we catch a glimpse of a crook-like bend in the river.

The sun beams down on the present kirk, which dates from the fourteenth century, and the fine houses in the Chanonry. On the far side of parkland, which now forms Seaton Park, a seventeenth-century mansion, Seaton House, can be seen. However, it was demolished in 1963 after being gutted by fire.

In 1495, King's College became the third university to be established in Scotland – after St Andrews and Glasgow. It was founded by William Elphinstone, Bishop of Aberdeen, with the backing of the Scottish king, James IV, and a Papal Bull. The original crown, similar to the imperial one that tops the spire of Edinburgh's St Giles Cathedral, blew down during a gale in 1633 but its replacement continues to dominate Old Aberdeen.

In 1593, a rival Reformed university was established in the new part of town and named after its founder, George Keith, fifth Earl Marischal of Scotland. In 1860, King's College and Marischal College united to become the University of Aberdeen.